IMPRESSIONS of

NORTHERN ENGLAND

Produced by AA Publishing

© AA Media Limited 2009

All rights reserved. No part of this publication may be reproduced, stored in
a retrieval system, or transmitted in any form or by any means – electronic,
photocopying, recording or otherwise – unless the written permission of the
publishers has been obtained beforehand.

Published by AA Publishing (a trading name of AA Media Limited, whose registered
office is Fanum House, Basing View,
Basingstoke, Hampshire RG21 4EA; registered number 06112600)

ISBN: 978-0-7495-6165-9

A04133

A CIP catalogue record for this book is available from the British Library.

Printed and bound in China by C & C Offset Printing Co. Ltd

Opposite: View across Thirlmere to Helvellyn, Lake District National Park, Cumbria.

IMPRESSIONS of

NORTHERN ENGLAND

Picture Acknowledgements

The Automobile Association would like to thank the following photographers, companies
and picture libraries for their assistance in the preparation of this book.

Abbreviations for the picture credits are as follows: (t) top; (b) bottom; (l) left; (r) right; (c) centre; (AA) AA World Travel Library.

3 AA/E A Bowness; 5 AA/C Lees; 7 AA/T Mackie; 8 AA/A J Hopkins; 9 AA/L Whitwam; 10 AA/T Mackie; 11 AA/L Whitwam; 12 AA/J Beazley; 13 AA/T Mackie; 14 AA/T Woodcock; 15 AA/S Day; 16 AA/P Bennett; 17 AA/T Mackie; 18 AA/T Mackie; 19 AA/R Coulam; 20 AA/T Mackie; 21 AA/T Mackie; 22 AA; 23 AA/T Mackie; 24 AA/T Mackie; 25 AA/L Whitwam; 26 AA/T Mackie; 27 AA/R Coulam; 28 AA/M Birkitt; 29 AA/T Mackie; 30 AA/T Mackie; 31 AA/T Mackie; 32 AA/S Day; 33 AA/T Mackie; 34 AA/P Baker; 35 AA/R Coulam; 36 AA/S Day; 37 AA/J Mottershaw; 38 AA/E A Bowness; 39 AA/E A Bowness; 40 AA/J Beazley; 41 AA/R Coulam; 42 AA/T Mackie; 43 AA/T Mackie; 44 AA/J Beazley; 45 AA/C Lees; 46 AA/G Rowatt; 47 AA/R Coulam; 48 AA/T Mackie; 49 AA/T Mackie; 50 AA/T Mackie; 51 AA; 52 AA/S Day; 53 AA/T Mackie; 54 AA/T Mackie; 55 AA/T Mackie; 56 AA/R Coulam; 57 AA/T Mackie; 58 AA/E A Bowness; 59 AA/R Coulam; 60 AA/S Day; 61 AA/L Whitwam; 62 AA/A J Hopkins; 63 AA/S Day; 64 AA/R Coulam; 65 AA/R Coulam; 66 AA/T Mackie; 67 AA/P Wilson; 68 AA/S Day; 69 AA/J Beazley; 70 AA/A Midgley; 71 AA/N Coates; 72 AA/T Mackie; 73 AA/T Mackie; 74 AA/A Midgley; 75 AA/R Coulam; 76 AA/R Coulam; 77 AA/R Coulam; 78 AA/T Mackie; 79 AA/R Coulam; 80 AA/L Whitwam; 81 AA/S Gregory; 82 AA/D Tarn; 83 AA/S Day; 84 AA/J Beazley; 85 AA/D Rowatt; 86 AA/R Coulam; 87 AA/R Coulam; 88 AA/T Mackie; 89 AA/J Beazley; 90 AA/R Coulam; 91 AA/R Coulam; 92 AA; 93 AA/M Trelawny; 94 AA/T Mackie; 95 AA/S&O Mathews; 96 AA/J Morrison; 97 AA/D Tarn; 98 AA/T Mackie; 99 AA/J Beazley; 100 AA/T Mackie; 101 AA/T Mackie; 102 AA/T Mackie; 103 AA/T Mackie; 104 AA/T Mackie; 105 AA/T Mackie; 106 AA/M Kipling; 107 AA/M Kipling; 108 AA/E A Bowness; 109 AA/T Mackie; 110 AA/E A Bowness; 111 AA/R Coulam; 112 AA/C Lees; 113 AA; 114 AA/T Mackie; 115 AA/J Morrison; 116 AA/T Mackie; 117 AA/T Mackie; 118 AA/R Coulam; 119 AA/T Mackie; 120 AA/T Mackie; 121 AA/P Sharpe; 122 AA/T Mackie; 123 AA/P Baker; 124 AA/R Coulam; 125 AA/R Coulam; 126 AA/D Tarn; 127 AA/R Coulam; 128 AA; 129 AA/R Coulam; 130 AA/T Mackie; 131 AA/T Mackie; 132 AA/M Kipling; 133 AA/M Kipling; 134 AA/S Day; 135 AA/D Tarn; 136 AA/R Coulam; 137 AA/T Mackie; 138 AA/M Kipling; 139 AA/M Kipling; 140 AA/R Coulam; 141 AA/T Mackie; 142 AA/R Coulam; 143 AA/P Wilson; 144 AA/T Mackie; 145 AA/T Mackie; 146 AA/M Birkitt; 147 AA/S&O Mathews; 148 AA/T Mackie; 149 AA/T Mackie; 150 AA/P Bennett; 151 AA/M Kipling; 152 AA/T Mackie; 153 AA/T Mackie; 154 AA/T Mackie; 155 AA/T Mackie; 156 AA/T Mackie; 157 AA/T Mackie; 158 AA/T Mackie; 159 AA/T Mackie.

Opposite: Antony Gormley's 'Angel of the North' stands on a hilltop above Gateshead.

INTRODUCTION

Topographically, culturally and historically the North of England is an area of great variety and contrasts. The rolling hills of Northumberland are totally different from barren emptiness of the Cumbrian fells, and while the west coast has golden sands and a mild climate, the east is famous for its rugged cliffs and bracing weather, and in contrast to the dramatic mountains of the Lake District, there is the gentle, pastoral scenery in the Limestone Dales.

Northern England changed dramatically during the 19th-century Industrial Revolution, with great conurbations developing around the coalfields and ports. Grand urban makeovers have transformed the cities of Manchester, Sheffield, Liverpool, Leeds and Newcastle into tourist attractions, drawing visitors for the stunning new buildings and magnificent museums and art galleries. You are never far from peaceful landscapes, pretty villages and stunning scenery – vast tracts of unspoilt, open country surround these cities.

The jewel in Northern England's crown is the Lake District in Cumbria. Despite its popularity, this magical corner of England retains an air of emptiness and remoteness, its craggy fells and peaceful lakes alive with the beauty that has inspired poets and writers like Wordsworth, Coleridge and Beatrix Potter. Escape the crowds by following remote paths and tracks through a dramatic landscape of soaring mountains, plunging waterfalls and remote tarns, or visit Wordsworth's Dove Cottage, take a leisurely cruise on Windermere, or negotiate the twists and turns of the spectacular Hardknott Pass.

Seaside, wild country and industry are rolled into one on Lancashire's coast and hinterland from Blackpool to the sweeping flat sands of Morecambe Bay, or the untamed wilderness of the Forest of Bowland.

Yorkshire is Britain's largest county, a vast and fascinating landscape with the magnificent medieval city of York, at the heart of Yorkshire and of England's history. The countryside is at its finest in the Dales and Moors. On the North York Moors, savage, desolate moorland, lush farmland and deep peaceful dales blend into an area of unique contrasts and beauty, where picturesque grey-stone villages are centres for magnificent walks by streams and waterfalls. The Dales is a striking limestone landscape of gorges, waterfalls, wide valleys, strange rock formations, potholes and miles of caves. Here, lush valley pastures give way to crags, grassland and moors on the hilltop. Don't miss Malham Cove and the austerely impressive scenery of Ribblesdale and Swaledale.

Northumberland, England's most northerly county, is a wilderness of outstanding and dramatic beauty: a lonely and unspoilt corner of England that is hard to equal. It is one of the few regions in Britain where you can still experience a tremendous sense of space and distance, walk for miles without meeting another soul and feel at one with the landscape. Explore the rolling Cheviot Hills and the secret valleys of the Tees and Wear, take in the hill-forts along the impressive and ancient Hadrian's Wall, and stroll along empty, unspoilt beaches dotted with castles.

Opposite: View over Ladybower Reservoir in the Peak District National Park, Derbyshire.

A wonderful panoramic view of the Peak District from Roaches Hill, Staffordshire.

The great choir of 13th-century Rievaulx Abbey, North York Moors National Park.

A frosty morning at Gunnerside in Swaledale, Yorkshire Dales National Park.
Opposite: Stunning reflections on a winter's day at Derwentwater.

Rural idyll at Pilsbury, Upper Dove Valley, Peak District National Park, Derbyshire.

'Amid the ivy', Tissington, Peak District National Park, Derbyshire.

The 13th-century keep of Warkworth Castle, Northumberland.

Ancient stone footbridge over Watendlath Beck, near Keswick, Lake District National Park, Cumbria.

The 18th-century mausoleum at Vanbrugh's Castle Howard, North Yorkshire.

Scots Pine trees reflected in Buttermere, Lake District National Park, Cumbria.

Colourful canal boats on the Peak District canal at Whaley Bridge, Peak District National Park, Derbyshire.
Opposite: The Millennium and Tyne Bridges in Newcastle-upon-Tyne, Tyne & Wear.

Springtime at Tideswell's 14th-century church of St John the Baptist, Peak District National Park, Derbyshire.

The fields and hills of Edale in the Peak District National Park, Derbyshire.

Sunset over Swinsty Reservoir, Washburn Valley, North Yorkshire.

Matlock's striking bell tower rises above the town centre, Peak District National Park, Derbyshire.

North Yorkshire's 12th-century Fountains Abbey is the best-preserved Cistercian Abbey in Britain.
Opposite: A late autumn morning in Little Langdale, Lake District National Park, Cumbria.

Old stone barn in the Manifold Valley, Peak District National Park, Staffordshire.

A patchwork of fields around Weardale, County Durham.

'Time for tea', Bakewell, Peak District National Park, Derbyshire.

The pond and stone buildings of Tissington village in the Peak District National Park, Derbyshire.

The curving staircase of a restored tram at the Crich Tramway Village, home of the National Tramway Museum.

Opposite: Detail of a 1904 Chesterfield Corporation tram, preserved and restored at the Crich Tramway Village, Matlock, Derbyshire.

A passing storm shower near Hawkshead, Lake District National Park, Cumbria.

Castlerigg Stone Circle in winter, near Keswick, Lake District National Park, Cumbria.

Flower beds in full bloom at Haddon Hall, Bakewell, Peak District National Park, Derbyshire.
Opposite: The Cheviots glow at sunset from Lordenshaws above Rothbury, Northumberland National Park.

Sun-lit fells reflect in the still waters of Thirlmere Reservoir, near Grasmere, Lake District National Park, Cumbria.

Dusk falls over Scarborough harbour, North Yorkshire.

The fertile Eden Valley, near Penrith, Cumbria.

Rowing on Grasmere, Lake District National Park, Cumbria.

The Royal Border Bridge, built between 1847-50, spans the River Tweed between Berwick-on-Tweed and Tweedmouth, Northumberland.

Rowing boats on the shore of Talkin Tarn, near Brampton, Cumbria.

View of Skiddaw and Derwentwater from Ashness Bridge, near Keswick, Lake District National Park, Cumbria.

Detail of a dry-stone wall in the Peak District National Park, Derbyshire.

Looking along Hadrian's Wall towards Housesteads Crag from Cuddy's Crag, Northumberland National Park.

The memorial to the Battle of Flodden Field (1513), Branxton, Northumberland.

A house on a rocky whinstone crag near Craster, Northumberland.
Opposite: 'Tide's Out', Alnmouth beach, Northumberland.

View of soaring fells from Hardknott Castle Roman fort, near Eskdale, Lake District National Park, Cumbria.

Herdwick sheep, a traditional Cumbrian breed, Lake Distict National Park.

View over Ullswater from Hallin Fell, Lake District National Park, Cumbria.

St Mary's Lighthouse stands on the rocky Tyne & Wear coastline at Whitley Bay.

Looking across the River Derwent to Cromford, Peak District National Park, Derbyshire.
Opposite: Sun setting over Eskdale, viewed from Hardknott Pass, Lake District National Park, Cumbria.

Ironwork detail on bandstand railings in the Pavilion Gardens at Buxton, Peak District National Park, Derbyshire.

Waterfall cascading from an ornamental lake in the Pavilion Gardens at Buxton, Peak District National Park, Derbyshire.

Poppies add a splash of colour to a 'field of gold', Northumberland.

Langdale Pikes from Great Langdale, Lake District National Park, Cumbria.

Rydal Mount, Wordsworth's home (1813-1850), Grasmere, Lake District National Park, Cumbria.

Castellated walls surround the beautiful Italianate gardens at Chillingham Castle, Northumberland.

Neolithic Castlerigg Stone Circle stands beneath towering fells near Keswick, Lake District National Park, Cumbria.

The rocky shoreline at Robin Hood's Bay, North York Moors National Park.

Brindley Water Mill reflected in its millpond, Leek, Staffordshire.
Opposite: View across Grasmere, Lake District National Park, Cumbria.

The River Tees rushes through Cauldron Snout below Cow Green Reservoir, County Durham.

A fish supper for a puffin on the Farne Islands, Northumberland.

Thor's Cave in the Manifold Valley, Peak District National Park, Staffordshire.

The 400-feet high chalk cliffs near Bempton, East Yorkshire.

Autumnal reflections in the waters of Watendlath Tarn, near Keswick, Lake District National Park, Cumbria.

Sheep grazing on the Cheviot Hills, Northumberland National Park.

Trees frame Closegate Bridge near Marsden, West Yorkshire.
Opposite: A stunning Peak District view from Mam Tor, near Castleton, Derbyshire.

Nora Battie's tea room sign on the Last of the Summer Wine *set in Holmfirth, West Yorkshire.*

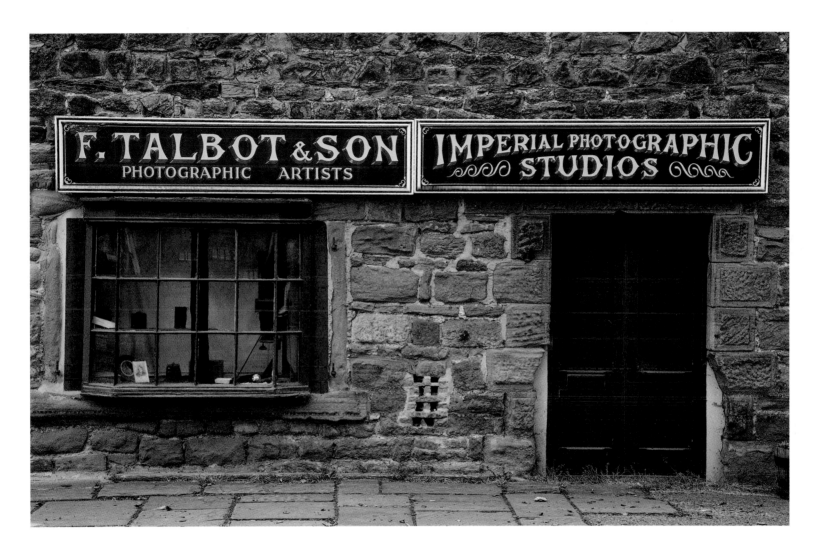

Recreation of the 1900s Fox Talbot shopfront at the Crich Tram Museum, Derbyshire.

The Emperor Fountain at Chatsworth House, near Bakewell, Peak District National Park, Derbyshire.

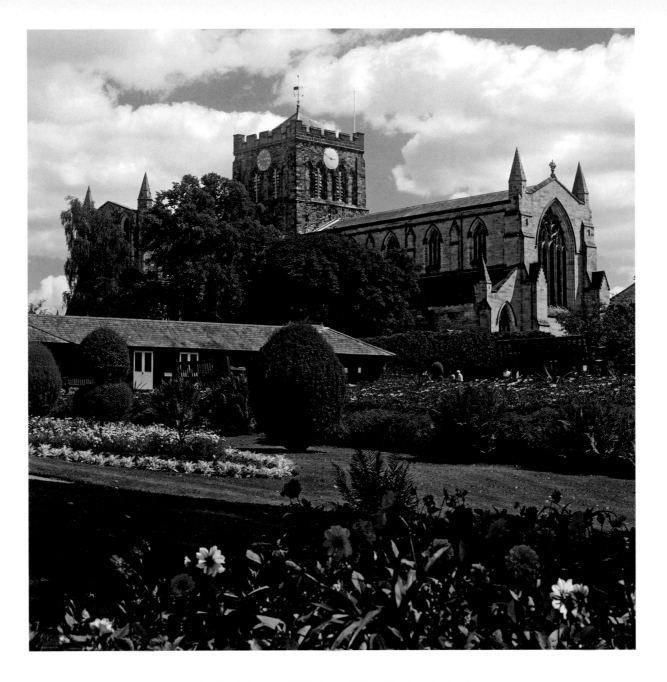

A colourful view of Hexham Abbey, Northumberland.

Birdoswald, an intact section of Hadrian's Wall, Northumberland.

Detail of old carved gravestone in St Cuthbert's churchyard, Bewcastle, Cumbria.

Topiary and gardens at Levens Hall, Kendal, Cumbria.

Opposite: Unusual wooden bridge at Hareshaw Dene, near Bellingham, Northumberland National Park.

The 18th-century rose window at Durham Cathedral, County Durham.

Georgian three-bay stone houses at Appleton-le-Moors, North York Moors National Park.

The Settle-Carlisle railway crosses the Dent Head viaduct in the glorious Yorkshire Dales National Park.

Hazy summer's day on Lake Windermere at Waterhead, Lake District National Park, Cumbria.

The Union Bridge across the River Tweed at Norham, Northumberland.

View of the Upper Coquet Valley at Alwinton, Northumberland National Park.

Detail of the Tyne Bridge, Newcastle-upon-Tyne, Tyne & Wear.
Opposite: The Sage Gateshead building and the Millennium and Tyne Bridges, Newcastle-upon-Tyne, Tyne & Wear.

A bleak valley scene in remote Snake Pass, Peak District National Park, Derbyshire.

Setting sun over the River Dove, Peak District National Park.

Old red post box set in a wall in Allenheads, Northumberland.

Victorian Cragside House, Rothbury, Northumberland.

View to Housesteads Crag from Cuddy's Crag on Hadrian's wall, Northumberland National Park.

The Bridestones, oddly-shaped gritstone rocks on the moors above Todmorden, West Yorkshire.

Ivy-clad stone cottage in Ashford-in-the-Water, Peak District National Park, Derbyshire.
Opposite: The River Breamish flowing through the Cheviot Hills in Northumberland.

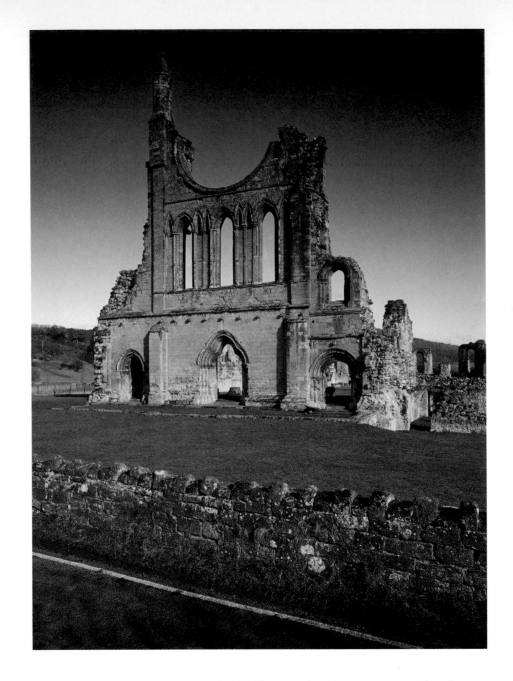

The ruins of 12th-century Byland Abbey, North York Moors National Park.

The vaulted 12th-century cellarium at Cistercian Fountains Abbey, Ripon, Yorkshire Dales National Park.

View over Morecambe Bay from Humphrey Head Point, near Grange-over-Sands, Cumbria.

The River Allen, Allen Banks, Northumberland.

An autumnal scene in Rosthwaite, Lake District National Park, Cumbria.

Looking down on Matlock Bath, Peak District National Park, Derbyshire.

Misty morning hike at Buttermere, Lake District National Park, Cumbria.

Opposite: Ladybower Reservoir in the Derwent Valley, Peak District National Park, Derbyshire.

Cowbar Cottage and fishing coble, Staithes, North Yorkshire.

View across Whitby's inner harbour at high tide, North Yorkshire.

The Langdale Pikes soar above Elterwater, Lake District National Park, Cumbria.

Winter morning view over Windermere from Orrest Head, Lake District National Park, Cumbria.

Dry-stone walling in Langdale, Lake District National Park, Cumbria.
Opposite: Arched bridge spanning the River Irthing at Lanercost, Cumbria.

Sea birds have colonised Marsden Rock, a 100-foot limestone stack off the Tyne & Wear coast.

Sailing on Errwood Reservoir in the golden sunlight, Peak District National Park, Derbyshire.

Pretty stone cottages at Grindleford, Peak District National Park, Derbyshire.

Hawes church in Wensleydale, Yorkshire Dales National Park.

A bright orange sunrise over Ribblehead, Yorkshire Dales National Park.
Opposite: The lush rural landscape around Muker, Yorkshire Dales National Park.

Dove Crag in the Simonside Hills, Rothbury, Northumberland National Park.

View across Wharfedale and the market town of Otley from Chevin Ridge, Yorkshire Dales National Park.

View of the River Swale at Gunnerside, Yorkshire Dales National Park.

Crummock Water, Lake District National Park, Cumbria.

Detail of an arched door at Knaresborough Castle, Yorkshire Dales National Park.

The idly-flowing River Wye at Bakewell, Peak District National Park, Derbyshire.

Rocky cliffs at Holwick Scar in the Upper Tees Valley, County Durham.

Foxgloves by a dry-stone wall in Teesdale, County Durham.

The amazing rock formations at Brimham Rocks in Nidderdale, Yorkshire Dales National Park.

Opposite: Antony Gormley's iconic iron sculpture, the 'Angel of the North', above Gateshead, Tyne & Wear.

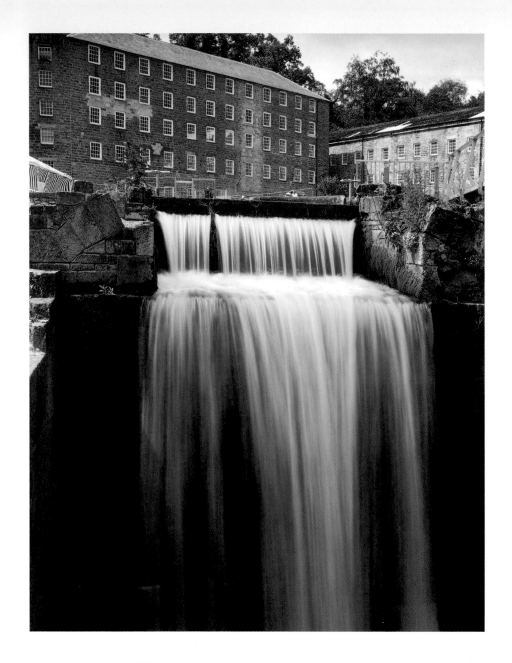

Dramatic waterfall at Cromford Mill, Peak District National Park, Derbyshire.

Rocky escarpment at Kinder Downfall, Peak District National Park, Derbyshire.

View across Robin Hood's Bay from Stoop Brow, Ravenscar, North York Moors National Park.

The view down New Road in the village of Robin Hood's Bay, North York Moors National Park.

Swans feed among the reeds on the still surface of Rydal Water, Lake District National Park, Cumbria.
Opposite: The dramatic Hawes to Thwaite road above Swaledale, Yorkshire Dales National Park.

Ferns growing beside the stream in Hareshaw Dene, north of Bellingham, Northumberland National Park.

Chocolate box-pretty stone cottage near Matlock, Peak District National Park, Derbyshire.

Looking across the jumble of cottages at Staithes from Cowbar, North York Moors National Park.

Kettleness headland from the Cleveland Way path, North Yorkshire.

Crammell Waterfall on the River Irthing near Gilsland, Cumbria.

White aconites growing in a wood in Miller's Dale, Peak District National Park, Derbyshire.

Lighthouse on Spurn Head at the mouth of the River Humber, East Riding of Yorkshire.
Opposite: View across cornfields to the Simonside Hills, near Whitton, Northumberland National Park.

Pine trees reflecting in Howden Reservoir, Peak District National Park, Derbyshire.

Trees and rhododendrons frame Howden Reservoir Dam, Peak District National Park, Derbyshire.

Fields near Chelmorton, Peak District National Park, Derbyshire.

Traditional hay meadows below Kisdon Hill near Muker in Upper Swaledale, Yorkshire Dales National Park.

Cascading water at West Burton Falls, Wensleydale, Yorkshire Dales National Park.

Stone bridge at Muker in Swaledale, Yorkshire Dales National Park.

The grand East Window at York Minster Cathedral, North Yorkshire.

View across Robin Hood's Bay from Ravenscar, North York Moors National Park.

Harvest time near Pateley Bridge, Yorkshire Dales National Park.
Opposite: Waterfall in Dentdale, Yorkshire Dales National Park.

A well in Ashford-in-the-Water, used in the traditional ceremony of Well Dressing, Peak District National Park, Derbyshire.

Bakewell's prominent church spire dominates the town and surrounding countryside, Peak District National Park, Derbyshire.

A stormy sky clouds the view across the Derwent Valley from Curbar Edge, Peak District National Park, Derbyshire.

Paved path to the summit of Mam Tor, Peak District National Park, Derbyshire.

Evening light bathes the landscape at Ingleborough, Yorkshire Dales National Park.

View over Semer Water in the Yorkshire Dales National Park.

INDEX